NEW APPRECIATIONS IN
HISTORY 20

Tudor Government

A. G. R. Smith

The Historical Association
59a Kennington Park Road, London SE11 4JH

Acknowledgements

The picture on the front cover, repeated on page 17, is reproduced by permission Copyright The Frick Collection.

The picture on page 4 is reproduced by permission of the Society of Antiquaries of London.

The pictures on pages 15, 20 and 21 are reproduced by permission of the National Portrait Gallery, London.

The picture on page 16 is reproduced by permission Thyssen-Bornemisza Collection, Lugano Switzerland.

This pamphlet has been edited by Bernard Capp

The publication of a pamphlet by The Historical Association does not necessarily imply the Association's official approval of its contents.

The Historical Association, founded in 1906, brings together people who share an interest in, and love for, the past. It aims to further the study and teaching of history at all levels: teacher and student, amateur and professional. Membership offers a range of over 100 publications available at very preferential rates, journals at generous discounts and also gives access to courses, conferences, tours, and regional and local activities. Full details are available from The Secretary, The Historical Association, 59a Kennington Park Road, London SE11 4JH, telephone: 071-735 3901

Designed and prepared by Colin Barker

©A.G.R. Smith, 1990, Reprinted 1992

ISBN 0 85278 327 2

Originated and published by The Historical Association, 59a Kennington Park Road, London SE11 4JH and printed in Great Britain by The Chameleon Press Limited, 5-25 Burr Road, London SW18 4SG.

Contents

The Aims of Government, Page 6

The Structure of Government, Page 7

The Nature of Government, Page 25

Success or Failure? Page 27

Notes, Page 31

Bibliography, Page 35

William Paulet, marquess of Winchester

His long tenure of the Lord Treasurership (1550-72) saw important reforms in royal land administration and significant increases in customs revenue, but his precise role in these and in the Exchequer reforms of the period has not yet been fully elucidated.

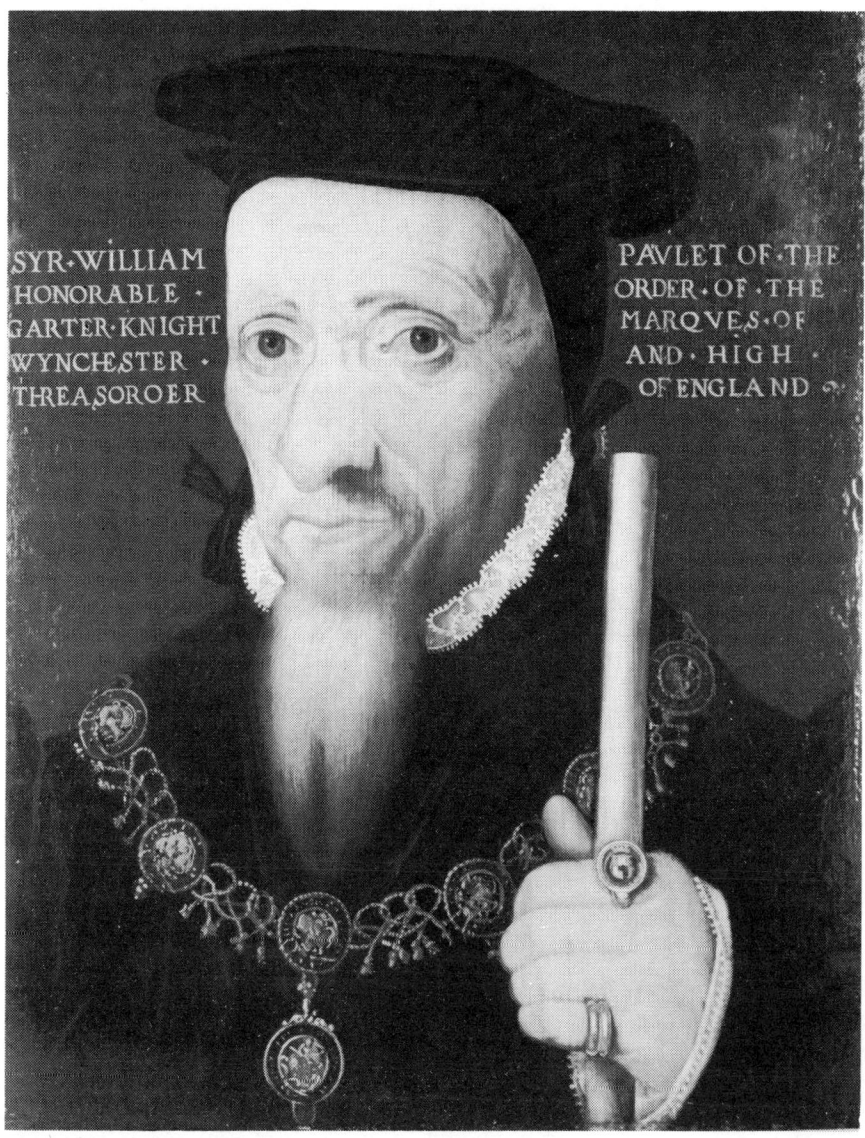

Tudor Government

On 21 August 1485 Henry Tudor won the battle of Bosworth in Leicestershire and established himself as Henry VII, king of England. He had landed in Wales two weeks before, the Lancastrian claimant to the throne against the incumbent Yorkist, Richard III. He had received assistance from Charles VIII of France and his invasion attracted English support as he marched across the country to his encounter with Richard at Bosworth. In the battle itself Richard tried to decide the issue by killing Henry in personal combat. Instead, he was killed himself, fighting bravely to the last. Bosworth seemed at the time a mere incident in 'the wars of the roses', that great dynastic struggle between the houses of Lancaster and York which plagued England from the 1450s onwards, but nearly 118 years later, on 24 March 1603, Henry's granddaughter Elizabeth died quietly in her palace at Richmond, in secure possession of the Crown which Henry had won so long before. Her successor, James VI of Scotland, acceded peacefully to the throne, riding south to take possession of his new kingdom amidst general rejoicing.

These descriptions of the birth and of the end of the Tudor regime suggest a transition from instability to stability. The regime was founded in battle and upheaval. It ended with a peaceful death and an unchallenged succession. That theme of stability will appear prominently in the discussion which follows, a discussion which will explore the aims, structure and nature of Tudor government and will conclude with an assessment of the extent of its success.

The Aims of Government

Any consideration of Tudor government must include the Church as well as the state. In the sixteenth-century Church and state were each regarded as including the whole of society, viewed from two different angles. The duty of the Church, the government and salvation of men's souls, was theoretically more important than that of the state, the government of men's bodies. The most fundamental of the duties of any Tudor regime was, therefore, the salvation of the souls of English men and women. The Church's obligation was to ensure that salvation by teaching right doctrine and by bringing the sacraments to the people. Also, in conjunction with the state authorities, it had to make sure that men adhered to the Church's teachings. Before the 1530s that responsibility fell upon the Church *in* England, the two provinces of Canterbury and York, which were theoretically independent of lay control, part of the universal Church of western Christendom, and subject to the overriding authority of the Papal Curia in Rome. From the 1530s, following the Henrician Reformation, it was the task of the Church *of* England, now a national institution headed by the sovereign, who had responsibility both for the doctrine and administration of the Church in his dominions.

Another fundamental aim of Tudor government was to defend the rights and maintain the status of the Crown. That duty inevitably involved European comparisons — the English sovereign's role and lifestyle were bound to be judged in relation to those of other European monarchs. This was very obvious, for example, in the area of Court life, where the elaborate pomp of the Papal Court, the glitter of the French Court, and the solemn protocol of the Spanish Court were all exemplars during the course of the sixteenth century. In the Tudor period, therefore, besides the defence of all the traditional prerogatives of the Crown, inherited from the middle ages, English sovereigns saw their status as bound up with the support of a splendid court. From the 1530s onwards they also — with the exception of the Catholic Mary — saw their rights and duties as including the government, in all its aspects, of the Church of England.

Tudor monarchs had too an obligation to keep the peace within the realm, always a fundamental task of any government. This included the discovery and defusing of potential and the suppression of actual rebellions; the maintenance of the general support of the 'political nation' — which basically consisted of those members of the aristocracy and gentry who administered the realm under the direction of the sovereign; and at least minimal care and concern for the 'lower orders', the poorer members of society, in times of dearth. Hunger could provoke unrest, and Tudor governments attempted to defuse the discontents of the poor by such measures as regulation of the food supply and the creation of a national system of poor relief.

Tudor sovereigns also had to defend the realm against actual or potential invasion by foreign powers, another fundamental task of government at any period in history. In the sixteenth century such invasions threatened from across the Scottish border — mounted either by the Scots alone or with the help of continental allies, from Ireland, and from the continent. This basic duty of defence against external threats was given added point from the 1530s onwards by the Reformation in England, with the ideological slant which it gave to the country's relations with European powers. England now seemed especially at risk from a possible crusading alliance between the two great Catholic powers of the continent, France and Spain, if only they could settle their own differences for long enough to mount an attack on schismatic England.

Tudor governments had in addition to raise enough money to achieve the objectives which we have already considered. During the first half of the century Henry VII and Henry VIII substantially boosted traditional sources of revenue or found new ones. Henry VIII in particular, by confiscating the lands of the monasteries during the 1530s and subsequently selling many of them, was able greatly to increase the revenue of the Crown in the short term. He also debased the coinage, and debasements and sales of former church lands continued in the reign of Edward VI. The greater part of these windfalls for the Crown was dissipated in the wars of the 1540s and 1550s and Elizabeth, when she came to the throne, depended much more upon policies of economy which inevitably included a determination to avoid large-scale and expensive wars if at all possible.

Tudor monarchs and ministers also took a 'paternalistic' interest in the welfare of the poorer sections of the community. That interest, as we have seen, partly reflected their concern for domestic peace, but it would be wrong to define it in such terms alone. Christian and humanistic influences, which stressed the duty of the better-off to aid and comfort the poor, were also strong, and the provisions of private charity and the terms of the evolving Tudor poor law demonstrated the genuine concern of the governments and governing classes of the time for the 'deserving' poor, those whose poverty was clearly no fault of their own.

In the broadest sense these aims, taken together, reflected a desire to achieve and preserve stability, always, of course, in the context of correct government of the Church, of the preservation of the rights of the Crown, and of the maintenance of the traditional social hierarchy, however precisely these might be defined at any given moment in time. The 'correct' government of the Church, for example, seemed a very different matter to Henry VII on the one hand and to Henry VIII in the later years of his reign, on the other.

The Structure of Government

The machinery of Tudor government existed to achieve the aims which have just been discussed. At its head were the sovereign and the Court. Tudor monarchy was limited. It was generally accepted that the wearer of the Crown was subject not only to God but also to the law.[1] In 1559 John Aylmer, later bishop of London, wrote that 'the regiment of England is not a mere monarchy, as some for lack of consideration think, nor a mere oligarchy, nor democracy, but a rule mixed of all these. ... It is not in England so dangerous a matter to have a woman ruler as men take it to be. For ... it is not she that ruleth but the laws. ... She maketh no statutes or laws, but the honourable court of Parliament'. About thirty years later Richard Hooker in his great work, *Of the Laws of Ecclesiastical Polity*, said much the same thing when he wrote that, 'though no manner person or cause be unsubject to the king's power, yet so is the power of the king over all and in all limited that unto all his proceedings the law itself is a rule'.[2]

Tudor sovereigns, then, were subject to the law. That, however, still left them very far above their subjects. Sir Thomas Smith, a distinguished servant of the Crown and the author of the best contemporary treatise on Tudor government, *De Republica Anglorum*, written in the 1560s, gave a good impression of the awe in which the monarch was held when he wrote, 'the prince is the life, the head and the authority of all things that be done in the realm of England. And to no prince is done more honour and reverence than to the king and queen of England; no man speaketh to the prince nor serveth at the table but in adoration and kneeling; all persons of the realm be bareheaded before him'.[3] Even experienced courtiers might be struck dumb in the presence of the sovereign. Michael Hickes, secretary to Lord Burghley, was a man who knew all the highways and byways of court life and most of the great men of the late Elizabethan period, but when, in 1597, he received the honour of a visit from the Queen at his country house in Essex, he was quite overcome by the greatness of the occasion. He had intended to make a speech of welcome to his royal guest but, as he later lamented to his friend Sir John Stanhope, a prominent courtier, 'the resplendence of her Majesty's royal presence and princely aspect did on a sudden so daunt all my senses and dazzle mine eyes as, for the time, I had use neither of speech nor memory'. He added that he took comfort from the fact that 'men of great spirit and very good speech have become speechless in the like case as men astonished and amazed at the majesty of her presence'.[4]

The aura of majesty which surrounded the monarch was, in theory, independent of the sovereign's personal qualities, but when it came to the practical business of ruling the prince's age, sex and personality were crucial. Edward VI ascended the throne as a boy of nine and his minority provided the opportunity for bitter rivalry between the dukes of Somerset and Northumberland for effective supremacy in the realm, a contest for power which dominated much of the reign. The young king showed a precocious intelligence and had strongly Protestant religious views, but, whatever his influence in some of the details of government,[5] it is difficult to see him as more than a well-informed puppet in the hands of his advisers. His half-sisters Mary and Elizabeth had the advantage of succeeding to the throne as adults but the disadvantage of being women. There was almost universal male prejudice at the time against female rulers. John Knox, in his *First Blast of the Trumpet Against the Monstrous Regiment of Women*, published in 1558, expressed that prejudice in intemperate terms when he wrote that 'to promote a woman to bear rule, superiority, dominion or empire above any realm, nation or city is repugnant to nature; contumely to God, a thing most contrary to his revealed will and approved ordinance'. He supported his argument from the Bible, the Fathers and the Classics and concluded that men were less than the beasts of the fields to permit such an inversion of God's intended order, 'for no man ever saw the lion make obedience and stoop before the lioness, neither yet can it be proved that the hind takes the conducting of the herd amongst the harts'.[6] Mary worked hard at state business but her limited political abilities, highlighted by her poor health throughout her reign, were grist to Knox's mill. Elizabeth, however, who, notoriously, was infuriated by the *Blast*, showed that a woman ruler *could* be successful. Highly intelligent, with the ability to pick good ministers and stand by them in adversity — Burghley and

Walsingham are the most notable examples — she founded her success, as Dr Haigh has so persuasively argued,[7] not by attacking the sixteenth-century stereotype of women as inferior to men but by accepting and at the same time escaping from it, arguing that she was no ordinary woman but a special instrument set aside by God to fulfil his divine purpose. The proof, Elizabeth argued, lay in her successes, which she interpreted as a sign of God's favour. As she told her last parliament in 1601, 'It hath pleased God ... by many hard escapes and hazards, both of diverse and strange natures, to make me an instrument of his holy will in delivering the state from danger and myself from dishonour'.

Henry VII and Henry VIII had the advantage of being adult and male when they ascended the throne and it is well known that Henry VII probably worked harder at the details of the business of monarchy than any other English sovereign before or since. The long lonely hours which he spent looking over his financial accounts were not, however repeated by his successor. Henry VIII, despite an unconvincing attempt to depict him in that role,[8] was not a diligent administrator. He left most of the details of government to his ministers, notably Wolsey and Cromwell, though he did intervene with brutal finality if his servants displeased him, as both Wolsey and Cromwell found to their cost, the former in 1529 and the latter in 1540.

Monarchs operated within the Court, centred on the royal palaces, where they were attended by their 'courtiers', well defined by Sir Geoffrey Elton as 'all those who at any given time were within "his grace's house", and all those with a right to be there'.[9] The Court was both a splendid setting for the monarch and the centre of the government of the realm. All Tudor monarchs appreciated the need to maintain a glittering Court. Henry VII may have been careful with money but he put on a fine show in his palaces, and the Yeomen of the Guard, founded in 1485, made a colourful military display in their distinctive uniforms. Henry VIII's reign saw the creation in 1539-40 of a new, even more colourful royal bodyguard, the gentlemen pensioners. Also during the 1530s the king, now head of the Church as well as the state, began to assume the title of majesty instead of the previous highness or grace. It was, in part at least, a symbol of his new status as ruler of an English 'nation state', subject to no external authority. The splendours of the Elizabethan Court, generally recognized as one of the most magnificent and ceremonious in Europe, are well brought out by Lupold von Wedel, a German nobleman who visited England in the 1580s and left a most interesting description of the country, including this account of the Queen in state:

> On the 18th [of October 1584] we walked a mile between walls which surrounded two gardens and which reach as far as Hampton Court, where the Queen resides. As it was Sunday we went to the church or chapel which is in the palace. This chapel is well decorated with a beautiful organ, silver gilt, with large and small silver pipes. Before the Queen marched her lifeguard, all chosen men, strong and tall, two hundred in number we were told, though not all of them were present. They bore gilt halberts, red coats faced with black velvet in front and on the back they wore the Queen's arms silver gilt. Then came gentlemen of rank and of the Council, two of them bearing a royal sceptre each, a third with the royal sword in a red velvet scabbard, embroidered with gold and set with precious stones and large pearls. Now came the Queen, dressed in black ...; on each side of her curly hair she wore a

9

large pearl of the size of a hazelnut. The people standing on both sides fell on their knees, but she showed herself very gracious, and accepted with an humble mien letters of supplication from rich and poor. Her train was carried behind her by a countess, then followed twelve young ladies of noble birth, children of counts or lords. ... Both sides of the gallery as far as the Queen walked through it to the chapel were lined by the guard bearing arms. As the day was almost gone there was no sermon, only singing and delivering prayers. Then the Queen returned as she had come and went to her room, and when on her passing the people fell on their knees, she said ...: 'thank you with all my heart'. Now eight trumpeters clad in red gave the signal for dinner and did it very well. Afterwards two drummers and a piper made music according to the English fashion, and we betook ourselves to our lodgings.[10]

Such pompous ceremonies, which so impressed both foreign visitors and the Queen's own subjects, were the public face of the Court. Behind the splendid facade, however, the royal palaces were the focal point of the government of the realm. Dr David Starkey has recently demonstrated the importance of their physical layout.[11] In particular he has emphasized the importance of the Privy Chamber, a set of private apartments created by Henry VII, probably in 1495, and closed to all but a handful of courtiers. The Eltham Ordinances of 1526, which described the new structure of the Court, divided it into three departments, Household, Chamber, and the new Privy Chamber, instead of into the traditional two, Household and Chamber. What mattered to courtiers, Starkey argues, was not so much the right to come to Court, but the right of access to the Privy Chamber, where alone a man could come into informal contact with the sovereign. Moreover, Tudor monarchs had different attitudes about ease of access to the Privy Chamber. Henry VII and Elizabeth were, says Starkey, 'distant' monarchs, who strictly limited access to their Privy Chambers. Henry VIII on the other hand was a 'participative' monarch, who allowed much freer entry. Such differing attitudes to admission to the inner sanctum of the palace had obvious implications for the conduct of politics and Starkey argues that 'the private apartments of ... Henry VIII ... were both an alternative power centre to the Council Chamber and a hotbed of factional intrigue. Councillors and courtiers vied for supremacy, and insecurity became both a fact of life and an instrument of royal policy. None of this was true under Henry VII [or] Elizabeth. ... Then Chamber and Council went their separate ways'.[12] In these circumstances the Privy Chamber became a barrier to rather than the centre of faction and Elizabeth was better able to stand aside from and manipulate faction struggles.

This provides an important perspective on the situation at Court during the Tudor period. Whatever the truth of Dr Starkey's theories about 'distant' and 'participative' monarchs — and for this writer they carry considerable conviction — it is generally recognized that the Council, which met at Court, was the centre of government, the linchpin of the administrative system, while the faction struggles of the century have been receiving increasing attention from historians. These factional disputes were intimately bound up with the fact that all prominent men in the Tudor period sought a share of the Crown's patronage, either for themselves or for the clients who depended upon them. The Crown had a vast range of benefits at its disposal: grants of honour, notably peerages and knighthoods; a great array of offices in the court, judiciary, central and regional administrations, military and naval services, in the royal land administration, and from the 1530s (and in practice even before) high offices in the Church. There were also leases, on favourable terms, of Crown lands, grants of export licences and monopolies, and pensions and annuities.

The great majority of those who benefited from this stock of patronage came from the 'political nation', those men who at any one time took an informed interest in the government of the realm. It has been estimated that by the Elizabethan period they numbered about 2,500.[13] That is a well informed guess but it does give some idea of the potential number of Court clients in the later sixteenth century. They can be divided into two groups. The larger consisted of those members of the gentry class who had no claims to direct contact with the monarch together with a number of aspiring lawyers, merchants and other prominent townsmen. Between these men and the sovereign, the nominal source of all patronage, stood the second group, those courtiers — great officials or favourites — who had either direct access to the sovereign and could thus solicit clients' suits or else who, if they held high office, might personally dispose of a portion of the royal store of patronage. Lord Burghley, for example, could help clients both because of his direct access to Elizabeth as her principal minister throughout the period 1558 to 1598 and also because his offices as Master of the Court of Wards between 1561 and 1598 and Lord Treasurer between 1572 and 1598 gave him a personal right to appoint to a number of administrative posts.

The clients who surrounded a great man formed his faction. They expected him to use his influence on their behalf and at the same time, by their number and status, they indicated their patron's influence with the sovereign and thus his standing in the state. The basic objective of faction leaders, therefore, was to advance their own wealth and power and the ambitions of their followers. From the 1530s onwards these struggles were affected by the Reformation, which gave an ideological element to factional politics which had not been present before, with 'conservatives' such as the Duke of Norfolk and Bishop Gardiner and 'radicals' such as Thomas Cromwell and Archbishop Cranmer trying either to slow down or hasten the progress of the Reformation. Recent analyses of early Tudor politics by Sir Geoffrey Elton,[14] Professor Ives[15] and Dr Starkey[16] have placed factional conflicts at the very centre of their accounts and have revealed in some detail the part they played in such major episodes as the fall of Anne Boleyn, the Pilgrimage of Grace, the fall of Cromwell, and the accession to power of Somerset on the death of Henry VIII. Similarly, on the mid-Tudor period, the works of Dr Hoak[17] and Professor Loades[18] have revealed much detail about the factional conflicts of 1547-58, which centred on the dukes of Somerset and Northumberland during Edward VI's reign and on Bishop Gardiner and Lord Paget in the Marian period. As far as Elizabeth's reign is concerned, historians have long cited with approval the words of Sir Robert Naunton, who wrote an account of the Queen and her courtiers and ministers in the early years of the seventeenth century. 'The principal note of ... [Queen Elizabeth's] reign', he stated, 'will be that she ruled much by faction and parties which herself both made, upheld and weakened, as her own great judgment advised'.[19] The rivalry of Leicester and Burghley in the early years of the reign and of Essex and Robert Cecil in the 1590s have been used both to confirm and illustrate Naunton's words.

Not all historians, however, have been entirely happy at the stress now being laid on the significance of factional conflicts throughout the Tudor period. Dr Simon Adams, for example,[20] argues that 'there is a great danger of trivialising contemporary political disputes by considering them all to have been factional'. He prefers to adopt a 'strict' rather than a 'loose' definition of the term, stating that 'a faction was not the same thing as clientage; nor was it the exercise of patronage; nor was it the taking of sides on a major political issue: a faction was a personal following employed in direct opposition to another personal following'. A factional struggle 'could involve disputes over patronage or debates over matters of state, but its essence was a personal rivalry that overrode all other considerations'. On that basis he sees only two 'real' faction struggles in the later sixteenth century, those between Somerset and Northumberland in Edward VI's reign and between Essex and Robert Cecil in the 1590s. This thesis puts the whole question of sixteenth-century faction into the historical melting-pot and it will clearly provoke considerable discussion in the years ahead. There is, however, much to be said for a 'looser' definition which continues to stress the exercise of patronage and/or political and ideological considerations. It would be unfortunate and misleading to exclude the Paget-Gardiner and Burghley-Leicester rivalries from the factional struggles of the period.

In any event, whether we regard a minor courtier as a member of a great man's 'faction' or merely as his 'client', it is clear that the problems of suing for advancement at Court were often both considerable and humiliating. The possibility of ultimate reward clearly made the struggles worthwhile for many, but even the most ardent must often have echoed the sentiments of the poet Edmund Spenser, a member of Essex's faction at Elizabeth's Court, who knew what he was talking about when he wrote in his poem *Mother Hubbard's Tale*

Full little knowest thou that has not tried,
What hell it is, in suing long to bide:
To lose good days, that might be better spent;
To waste long nights in pensive discontent;
To speed today, to be put back tomorrow;
To feed on hope, to pine with fear and sorrow,
To have thy Prince's grace, yet want her Peer's;
To have thy asking, yet wait many years;
To fret they soul with crosses and with cares;
To eat thy heart through comfortless despairs;
To fawn, to crouch, to wait, to ride, to run,
To spend, to give, to want, to be undone. ...[21]

The Court, where suitors sought patronage and where high political decisions were made, was also, during most of the Tudor period, the meeting place of the Council. Until the 1530s the Council was a very large body. During Henry VII's reign as many as 40 councillors might be present at a meeting and in the early years of Henry VIII the size of the Council reached 70. In the 1530s there was a significant change when Thomas Cromwell created — probably in 1536 — a much smaller Privy Council of only 19 members, which in 1540 acquired its own staff and register. Numbers grew again under Edward VI and Mary, but the Elizabethan body was similar in size to the Cromwellian Council, with 19 members in 1559 reduced to only 14 at the end of the reign.

Throughout the Tudor period the Council had three main functions. It gave the sovereign advice, it was the central administrative body in the realm, and it exercised judicial (or quasi-judicial) functions. It tendered advice when asked and Lord Burghley expressed the classic advisory duty of a councillor when he told Robert Cecil in 1596; 'I do hold, and will always, this course in such matters as I differ in opinion from her Majesty; as long as I may be allowed to give advice I will not change my opinion by affirming the contrary, for that were to offend God, to whom I am sworn first; but as a servant I will obey her Majesty's commandment and no wise contrary the same, presuming that she being God's chief minister here, it shall be God's will to have her commandments obeyed, after that I have performed my duty as a councillor'.[22]

Though he Council's duty to advise the sovereign — often on matters of high policy — was the most dramatic aspect of its work, its most time-consuming preoccupation was with its routine administrative tasks. The Council registers reveal that it concerned itself with everything that went on in England. It exercised supervision over the economic and religious as well as over the political and administrative life of the country, and when war came it played the major role in organizing both offensive and defensive operations, as after 1585, when the great struggle against Spain added immensely to its already heavy workload. Its burdens were increased by the private suitors who bombarded it with pleas for assistance in injustices which they claimed to have suffered. The Privy Council was not, in the strictest technical sense, a court, but its concern with private suitors reflected its exercise of the sovereign's right — and duty — to see that justice was done to all the subjects of the realm, and Roger Windham, a Norfolk gentleman who was twice gaoled in the 1590s until he agreed to comply with a Council order, was only one of many who were made very well aware of the effective judicial authority which councillors exercised.[23]

The Privy Council, then, was undoubtedly the very centre of the government of England, and Dr Starkey has argued[24] that its affliation was with the Court rather than, as Sir Geoffrey Elton would have it, with the administrative departments of state. That seems too simple an argument. As we have seen, although the Privy Council *did* meet at Court its work was the superintendence of *all* the business of state. It thus provided the vital link between the sovereign and the Court on the one hand and the central bureaucracy and the localities on the other. It should be seen as *both* a Court institution *and* as part of the administrative machinery of the state, and that should indicate the difficulties of any attempt to separate too rigidly the Court and the administration.

The central administrative agencies which the Council superintended were often called courts and — though they frequently performed administrative as well as judicial duties — that reflected the fact that many organs of central government were concerned with the preservation of law and order and the punishment of evil doers, an indication both of the immense importance of the task and of the contemporary emphasis — itself an inheritance from the middle ages — on the sovereign as the dispenser of justice. Some were also intimately involved in other fundamental tasks of Tudor government, the raising of money, the defence of the realm, and the control of the Church. We cannot discuss here the work of Chancery, the Exchequer, the courts of King's Bench and Common Pleas and of other institutions which the Tudors inherited from the middle ages or the tasks of the courts of Star Chamber and High Commission, of the Navy Board and of other bodies established in the sixteenth century,[25] but it should be noted that a key role in the maintenance of both the domestic and foreign security of the realm was played by the secretary of state. This office was given a central role by Thomas Cromwell during the 1530s, when he had a hold on almost all the affairs of the realm, and, after some vicissitudes in the middle years of the century, it again reached great heights of importance during Elizabeth's reign when William Cecil, Francis Walsingham and Robert Cecil successively maintained it at the very heart of the machinery of government. At the end of the century Robert Cecil wrote of it 'All officers and counsellors of princes have a prescribed authority by patent, by custom or by oath, the secretary only excepted'. He had 'a liberty to negotiate at discretion at home and abroad ... all matters of speech and intelligence'.[26*] It was this general responsibility for the security of the realm which enabled Walsingham to build up his famous spy system, which played such a major role in securing useful foreign intelligence.[27]

The central institutions of government were staffed by official 'civil servants' who were paid a salary, generally very inadequate, by the state, but who depended, for the maintenance of a decent standard of living, on the fees which they received for prescribed administrative duties and on the gratuities which they often obtained from hopeful or grateful clients, anxious to ease their way through tangled administrative processes by securing the goodwill of those who worked in government offices. These civil servants were few in number, perhaps only about 1,200 in the later years of the century.[28] That was a small fraction of the 40,000 or 50,000 officers who served the French monarchy by the early seventeenth century, though many of them worked in regional and local government. However, in addition to the official civil servants many others worked in the English central government machine, often fulfilling very important roles. Professor Jones has shown how the great expansion of Chancery's work in the sixteenth century meant that its established officials were no longer able to handle all the business. As a result 'an overburdened official would begin to appoint his own personal assistants, responsible to him alone and engaged on his terms. They in turn would also appoint 'servants' to assist in the performance of their duties. A spectacular example of all this is provided by the Six Clerks [important Chancery officials], each of whom began to employ as many as ten underclerks. These in turn began to employ, and were assisted by, another range of subordinates'.[29]

Further insights into the workings of the central administration can be obtained if we examine the workings of Burghley's personal secretariat during the later years of

Henry VII

By bringing to an end the wars of the Roses he created a stable government.

Henry VIII and Thomas Cromwell

They brought about the break with Rome, thus endowing the Crown with the headship of the Church of England and creating an English 'nation-state' subject to no external authority.

his life. After 1572 he was no longer secretary of state, though he held the great offices of Lord Treasurer and Master of the Court of Wards, each carrying with it considerable patronage. His influence over the whole range of state business depended not on any specific office which he held but on the fact that he was the Queen's principal adviser. He continued even after he had resigned the secretaryship to concern himself with England's foreign relations and, while one of his two chief secretaries, Michael Hickes, dealt primarily with patronage, the other, Henry Maynard, involved himself in the business of countries ranging from Scotland to Germany. He performed these tasks as his master's private assistant both during Walsingham's tenure of the secretaryship of state and also after the latter's death in 1590, when the office remained vacant for six years and Burghley assumed informal responsibility for the work, assisted by Maynard and Robert Cecil. All this shows just how personal and 'unbureaucratic' administration could still be at the end of Elizabeth's reign.[30]

It is remarkable that this small and seemingly ramshackle government machine could at times produce considerable administrative achievements. One of the most notable of these was the *Valor Ecclesiasticus*, a statement of all the revenues of the Church, drawn up in 1535 by royal commissions which were set up for each shire. The huge task was completed in just over nine months and Professor Knowles, who made a happy comparison between the *Valor*'s importance for Tudor England and that of *Domesday Book* for the Norman period, drew attention to the vital interplay in its successful completion between the drive imparted by the central administration under Cromwell's direction and the work of the local commissions, composed mostly of 'amateur' gentlemen from the shires.[31] The composition of the *Valor*, in fact, is a commentary on one of the most important facts about Tudor government: it worked best, indeed it only really worked at all, when there was effective co-ordination and co-operation between the centre and the localities.

The central institutions of government and the personnel who manned them worked continuously at the business of government. Parliament, in contrast, was an occasional institution. It met only when the monarch summoned it and lasted for as long as he or she deemed necessary. There have been two major trends in the recent historiography of Tudor parliaments. One has been to play down their general importance, stressing their occasional nature. The other, in sharp contrast to the views of Sir John Neale, has been to see them as an integral part of government rather than as forums for opposition to the Crown. The revisionists, headed by Elton and Dr Michael Graves, do, of course, admit that there was opposition to specific government policies in many Tudor parliaments, in Henry VIII's reign as well as in that of Elizabeth, but they see these differences as part of the normal give and take of the political process and stress instead the extent of co-operation between the three elements in the parliamentary trinity, Crown, Lords and Commons. As a result of that co-operation the Lords and Commons granted necessary taxation to the sovereign, and Crown, Lords and Commons together passed a great mass of legislation, much of it of general public interest and importance but a good deal also of private significance, pertaining to the affairs and interests of specific localities and private gentlemen. In this new picture the House of Lords looms much larger than it did in Neale's story, where it appeared usually as a shadowy entity behind the forceful and articulate House of Commons.[32]

This revised picture, provided that it is not pushed so far as to diminish unduly the opposition which certainly existed to some Crown policies,[33] seems generally convincing. It certainly fits in well with informed contemporary views of parliament, notably those of Sir Thomas Smith, who stressed its legislative role. Every bill had to be accepted by Crown, Lords and Commons before it could become law, so that each piece of legislation 'is the prince's and whole realm's deed; whereupon justly no man can complain but must accommodate himself to find it good and obey it'.[34] Public legislation, by catering for the developing needs of the realm, helped to produce stability, as did private legislation, which addressed the needs of individual gentlemen. Members of the political nation thus saw meetings of parliament as useful occasions, as 'points of contact' between the centre and the localities, and Elton, in coining that happy phrase, has noted how, from the 1530s onwards, successive houses of Commons became nurseries for the ambitious or able men who wished to rise in the service of the state. From that decade onwards most Tudor privy councillors served an apprenticeship in the Commons.

The Church's parliaments were Convocations, separate meetings of the clergy of the provinces of Canterbury and York, but in 1532, with the 'submission of the clergy' to Henry VIII's authority, Convocations lost their independent legislative powers. From then onwards they were effectively at the mercy of the laity.

Parliaments and the central administrative machinery touched the lives of the great majority of sixteenth-century English men and women much less directly than the institutions of local government. For most of the people it was local officials, especially the ubiquitous justices of the peace, who determined their fate. When one remembers in addition the strength of local patriotism — a Tudor man who referred to his 'country' usually meant his native shire rather than the whole of England — it is clear that the details of county administration should loom large in any discussion of sixteenth-century government.[35]

In the Tudor period the sheriff, who had at one time been the most important local official in the shires, declined in importance: by Elizabeth's reign the office was generally an expensive and time-consuming honour without much effective power. On the other hand, the sixteenth century saw a considerable growth in the powers and duties of another medieval officer, the justice of the peace, and the creation of an important new office, that of lord lieutenant. The lieutenancy was essentially military in character and its tentative beginnings can be seen in the reign of Henry VIII, during the dangers of the Reformation years. In the later part of Edward VI's reign Northumberland seems to have

Elizabeth I and William Cecil, Lord Burghley

contemplated making the lieutenancy a permanent part of the administrative system but Mary and Elizabeth, in her early years, did not follow these precedents and until the 1580s lieutenants were temporary officials whose posts were granted for special reasons. From the 1580s, however, with the Spanish war, lieutenancies became a permanent feature in most English counties, though much of the work was done by deputies. Lieutenants' duties remained essentially military — they were responsible for assembling and training men for military service within their jurisdictions — but they had other duties too, for example they were responsible for the collection of the

Two arch-conservatives. During their 40 year partnership between 1558 and 1598 they maintained the stability of the English state, largely by refusing to make any significant governmental innovations.

loans which were raised on occasion by the Crown to meet extraordinary expenses. Their work was closely supervised by the Privy Council, to which they made full reports, and by the 1590s they formed a vital link between the central administration and the localities, representing the views of their shires to the Council and in turn, conveying its orders to their districts.[36]

Beneath the lord and deputy lieutenants were the justices of the peace, the key figures in local government. During the sixteenth century there was a great increase in their numbers and work. At the beginning of the Tudor period there were, on average, less than 10 justices per shire, by the middle of Elizabeth's reign the average was 40 or 50, and by 1603 numbers ranged from 50 to 90. That Elizabethan growth took place despite a number of 'purges' of the bench by Burghley, who believed in a relatively small number of hard-working justices in each county. His wishes were frustrated because, by the middle of the Tudor period, a seat on the bench was seen as a mark of social distinction and, despite the expansion in numbers, the bulk of the work in most counties continued to be done by a relatively limited number of individuals.

The minority of 'working' justices certainly had a greatly increased volume of business heaped upon their shoulders. William Lambarde, a Kentish lawyer and antiquary, gave an account of the justices' work at the end of the century in his *Eirenarcha*, the most famous Tudor treatise on the justices' office. In the 1599 edition he listed 306 statutes which required j.p.s' assistance for their enforcement. Of these only 133 predated 1485, 98 belonged to the period 1485-1558, and 75 were passed in Elizabeth's reign between 1559 and 1597.[37] Some of these Tudor statutes contained complex and important provisions — notably the Elizabethan statutes dealing with apprenticeship, the poor and vagrancy — but the burdens which they imposed, essentially administrative in nature, were only part of the justices' work. Their judicial duties were enshrined in the commission of the peace, issued each year, which gave them the right to hear and determine the widest variety of criminal cases, though their civil jurisdiction was limited. Some tasks could be undertaken by justices acting singly or in small groups but their principal work centred in quarter sessions which, as the name suggests, were held four times a year, with additional sessions when necessary.

Within each county were smaller units of local government, hundreds and parishes. The former still retained some importance at the end of the sixteenth century — justices often organized themselves by hundreds and lieutenants and their deputies carried out their musters hundred by hundred — but the parish was much more significant. Originally a unit of ecclesiastical government it increasingly became part of secular administration after the Reformation. Already before 1558 it was given a variety of responsibilities for poor relief, and in Elizabeth's reign it became a major unit of local administration. The Elizabethan legislation on the poor gave it an organized machinery for raising and administering a poor rate and it also became responsible for other duties, such as the relief of disabled soldiers and sailors. By 1603 it had a staff of constables, churchwardens, overseers of the poor and surveyors of roads.[38]

Tudor England was overwhelmingly a rural society and though the urban population rose from about 4% of the total in 1500 to 7% or 8% in 1600 only London, with 50,000 or 60,000 people in the earlier part of the century and about 200,000 at the end of Elizabeth's reign, was a substantial city. Most towns were effectively oligarchical in government, with a mayor and a limited number of aldermen controlling most aspects of town life.

The localities, whose institutional

framework we have just examined, were subjected to greatly increased pressures from the centre as the century progressed. Some indication of these pressures has already been given in noting the multiplicity of statutory burdens which had been placed on j.p.s by the second half of the century. Attempts to secure religious conformity and the problems associated with war also illustrate the Crown's increasing demands. From the 1570s onwards missionary priests from the continent made their way in increasing numbers to England with the objective of sustaining the faith of those Catholics who had remained loyal to the old Church and converting or reconverting others. This situation, in turn, led to increasing demands from the government that local magistrates should seek out and interrogate suspected recusants. More burdensome for local governors and local society were the substantial and virtually continuous demands made on the shires from 1585 until the end of Elizabeth's reign for contributions of men, money and arms for the war against Spain.[39]

Descriptions of the institutional framework of local government and comments upon the increasing pressure to which it was subject from the central authorities give valid impressions of the localities throughout much of England. It must be stressed, however, that, within that general picture, the situation in each county varied widely. That was true not only of the geography and economy of individual shires but also — the point which concerns us here — of their politics as well. That political diversity appears very clearly in Dr Alison Wall's recent survey of 'political patterns' in the localities.[40]

Many counties, including Kent, Norfolk, Suffolk, Herefordshire, Wiltshire and Northumberland, were rent by faction struggles, with ambitious county gentry attempting to secure the help of friends at Court in their struggles for local supremacy. Other shires, such as Hertfordshire, Leicestershire, Derbyshire, Lancashire, Durham, Cheshire, Sussex and Essex were more peaceful during the Elizabethan period, often because local magnates with exceptional court influence or dominant local power, or both, occupied virtually unchallengeable positions from which they were able to satisfy the ambitions of local gentlemen for office in the shires and access to court favours.

It is clear, therefore, that the workings of the patronage system, which spread its tentacles from the centre through the shires, was a vital element linking the Court on the one hand with the localities on the other. With no standing army and no large paid bureaucracy or effective police force in the localities the Crown was basically dependent on the goodwill of the majority of the political nation for enforcing its will. It relied, to some extent, in securing that good will, on moral exhortations — the homilies of obedience, so often declaimed from pulpits throughout the land, stressed the hierarchy of divinely instituted authorities which obliged lesser governors to support the sovereign[41] — and on superintendence from the centre, principally by the Privy Council but also by the judges on their assizes, their biannual tours of the shires to hear and determine important legal cases. Fundamentally, however, the Crown had to secure the co-operation of local gentlemen by appealing to their self-interest. These gentlemen needed opportunities to secure the prestige and material rewards which could only be effectively conferred by office and favour from the Crown, while at the same time they had to ensure that they remained on good terms with at least a cross-section of their fellow-gentlemen in the localities. That fundamental fact helps to explain why stark distinctions between 'Court' and 'country' are unhelpful when discussing Tudor government and society. Members of the gentry, if they were to be successful in their careers, had to keep a foot in each camp, to keep open lines of access to both court favours and to the goodwill of their fellow governors in the shires.

The gentlemen who ruled the counties had, in their turn, to secure the obedience of the lower orders, those below the traditional governing class who, as Sir Thomas Smith starkly and succinctly put it, 'have no voice nor authority in our commonwealth, and no account is made of them but only to be ruled'.[42] They too, just like their social superiors, were subjected from the pulpits of the realm to a constant barrage of homilies and sermons which urged them to obey cheerfully those lawfully set over them in accordance with God's divine plan. That obedience to their gentry rulers and through them to the sovereign was theoretically unconditional, but in fact there was an implicit bargain between rulers and ruled. The former were expected by their inferiors — and generally accepted the obligation — to do their utmost to secure a minimal standard of living for the poorer members of the community, especially in times of distress, notably plague, famine or war. The detailed stories of the development of the Tudor poor law[43] and of the restrictions which were constantly placed on grain exports at times of high prices[44] — stories which cannot be told here — are reflections of that obligation, an obligation founded not only on the gentry's fear of disturbances in the localities but also on what they regarded as their moral duty, based on Christian teaching and humanistic influences, to provide relief for the poorer of their fellow countrymen.

So far we have been concerned with the structure of secular government, but the administration of the Church must also receive brief attention. Before the Henrician Reformation the Church, as we have already noted, was part of the vast edifice of Catholic Christendom, theoretically independent in its most important functions of the state apparatus. It enjoyed a revenue perhaps three times as great as that of the Crown. By Elizabeth's reign it was a national institution, subject in both its doctrine and its government to the authority of the Queen in parliament, though Elizabeth endeavoured throughout her reign to keep the practical role of parliament to a minimum. For her the government of the Church rested, under her own superintendence, in Convocation, in the bishops and in the Court of High Commission, established in 1559 to exercise the Crown's delegated ecclesiastical supremacy. Some members of the Commons demanded a much greater role for parliament in Church affairs than the Queen was prepared to concede but, whatever judgment is made about the precise theoretical and practical roles of the Crown on the one hand and parliament on the other in control of the Church, it is beyond dispute that the Tudor period saw the 'triumph of the laity' over the clergy in ecclesiastical affairs. By 1603 a lay monarch — and a woman at that — and a parliament dominated in both Lords and Commons by the laity were between them the dominant voices in the government of a Church which in 1485 had been ruled by its own clergy. At the same time the Church as an institution had become immeasurably poorer; by the beginning of Elizabeth's reign its total income was probably less than half that of the Crown.

The Nature of Government

Our dissection of the structure of government has already thrown out hints about its nature, but now we will turn to the issue of 'Tudor despotism' and to the debate over a possible 'Tudor revolution in government'. The idea of Tudor despotism is based upon the argument that Henry VIII and Thomas Cromwell, buttressed by the new royal supremacy over the Church, tried to override limitations on the monarchy's secular authority and create an absolutism untrammelled by law. It was given its most notable recent statement in 1967 by Professor Hurstfield,[45] but Elton has strongly rejected it.[46]

It has already been noted that contemporary authorities agreed that the king was subject to the law, that the law could only be changed by the consent of the Lords and Commons in parliament, and that that consent could never be taken for granted throughout the Tudor period. Moreover, in his massive study of the enforcement of the Henrician Reformation in the localities[47] Elton has demonstrated that the government and Cromwell stuck rigidly to the letter of the law. The possibility remains that some laws, even though they were passed with parliamentary consent, were so dangerous to the traditional constitutional framework that they raised the possibility or perhaps even the reality of despotic rule. Professor Heinze has shown, however, that the Proclamations Act, which ordered that royal proclamations were to be obeyed as though they had been made by act of parliament, cannot legitimately be regarded as an instrument of despotism — it was concerned essentially with the practical difficulties of enforcing proclamations.[48] The treason legislation, which condemned men to death for mere words against the royal supremacy, and the acts of attainder, which ordered executions without due process in the courts, were certainly very harsh measures with tyrannical implications, but they were used against only a limited number of men and women — many of them members of the political nation — and were enforced through the normal institutions of central and local government. It is clear, in fact, that Henry VIII retained the general support of the vast majority of the aristocracy and gentry while he condemned a limited number of their fellows to the cruel death of traitors. If this was 'despotism', it was within the letter of the law, it was very limited in scope, and it was implemented with the active or tacit support of the vast bulk of the political nation. It seems best to avoid emotive words like 'tyranny' and 'despotism' and to say that in carrying out a revolution — the Reformation — Henry and Cromwell sometimes resorted to cruel, even savage, measures which were still within the law.

Most Tudor historians would probably agree with Elton in dismissing the idea of Tudor despotism, but many reject his thesis of a Tudor 'revolution in government', first propounded in 1953 in a famous book[49] and defended with great vigour ever since. His basic idea is that there was a fundamental change in the nature of Tudor administration in the 1530s. Before then, he argues, Tudor government was essentially 'household' government, an administrative system inherited from the middle ages in which the mainsprings of action lay in the royal household. After the 1530s, as a result of Thomas Cromwell's reforms of financial institutions, of the Council and of the Secretaryship, it was essentially modern 'bureaucratic' government, with great departments of state administering the realm largely independently of the monarch's personal actions.

Detailed criticism of Elton's thesis by Professor Wernham and by Drs Harriss and Williams came in the late 1950s and early 1960s[50] and since then other Tudor experts have either suggested significant modifications or else have rejected it altogether.[51] They have had much support from medievalists, like Professor Brown who recently wrote that 'it is ... a fundamental mistake to consider late medieval government "Household" government'. It was instead founded on three great Westminster offices headed by the chancellor, the treasurer and the keeper of the privy seal. 'These offices can justifiably be described as bureaucratic'.[52] If medievalists like Brown see fifteenth-century government as more 'bureaucratic' than Elton would allow, the most iconoclastic of his Tudor critics, Dr Starkey, stresses the continuing importance of the household throughout the Tudor period, or at least during the first half of the century.[53] Up until 1558, he argues, the Privy Chamber, the very centre of the household, was politically active and, at times, politically dominant. Only in Elizabeth's reign did it cease to be politically significant, and even that did not mean the end of the household's importance in the government of early modern England. In James I's reign another household department, the Bedchamber, rose to prominence, fulfilling many of the political roles of the early Tudor Chamber.

Another formidable critic of Elton, Dr Alsop, has pointed out the difficulties in distinguishing between so-called 'household' and 'bureaucratic' administrative methods[54] and Mr Coleman, in a detailed study of the Exchequer between 1554 and 1572[55] shows *inter alia* that the Receipt, the department of the Exchequer which handled cash, was reorganized four times during these years, that the complex processes of change which took place in it owed nothing to a supposed Cromwellian reforming ideology, and, indeed, that the then Lord Treasurer, the marquess of Winchester, Cromwell's supposed pupil and heir, was an arch-conservative who tried to re-establish in the Receipt what he thought to be twelfth-century practices.

These are formidable onslaughts on Elton's 'administrative revolution' and though, in face of them all, he still maintains the fundamentals of his interpretation,[56] it looks increasingly untenable. Even so, Cromwell's governmental work remains of formidable importance. His creation of a small, strong Privy Council, the dramatic increase in the importance of the secretaryship which took place during his ministry, his abolition of liberties and sanctuaries throughout England, his measures to increase central oversight of the northern and western parts of the realm, and his administrative union of England and Wales, together with the subordination of the Church to the state which accompanied these measures, were crucial in the creation of a unitary realm with limited but effective central institutions. That was one of the great achievements of Tudor history and it is for his role in it rather than in any imaginary revolution in governmental methods that Cromwell deserves his fame as an administrator.

Success or Failure?

Historians, who have vigorously disagreed about the nature of Tudor government, have also differed about the extent of its successes and failures. These can be discussed in two ways. They can be assessed in terms of the specific aims of Tudor governments and they can also be analysed in a more general way in the context of the strength (or weakness) of the Tudor regime as a whole.

As far as specific aims are concerned Tudor governments were not able to ensure that all men and women followed the official doctrine of the state church, whatever that was at any specific moment. At the end of the century, over forty years after the Elizabethan settlement, there were Catholics who rejected the whole idea of the Reformation and Separatists who rejected the concept of a state church to which all should belong. Nevertheless, by 1603 the Church of England had established itself in the life of the nation and had been provided with defensible disciplinary, doctrinal and philosophical bases. The speed at which Protestantism took root among the population from the 1530s onwards has been much disputed — Professor Dickens stresses relative rapidity and Dr Haigh relative slowness[57] — but there can be little doubt that by 1603 the process was well advanced.

Tudor monarchs, always at the centre of a splendid Court, greatly raised their status by subordinating the Church to the Crown and thus creating both an imperial kingship and a new kind of English state subject to no external authority. They thus launched England (and later Britain) on a constitutional path which was basically followed until 1973 when adherence to the E.E.C. once more subordinated the realm to the rulings of a foreign institution. Within this new sixteenth-century nation-state governments tried hard to keep the peace by anticipating and preventing potential plots and rebellions. Sometimes, as when Walsingham uncovered the Babington plot in 1586, they were successful. When revolts *did* break out — as for example in 1487 (Lambert Simnel), in 1536 (The Pilgrimage of Grace), in 1549 (the West Country and East Anglian revolts), in 1553 (the attempt to put Lady Jane Grey on the throne), in 1554 (Wyatt's rebellion), in 1569 (the revolt of the Northern Earls), and in 1601 (Essex's rebellion) — they were always suppressed; the only successful rebellion in England between 1485 and 1603 was that of Henry VII himself when he won the throne at Bosworth.

Tudor governments also successfully defended the realm against foreign powers. The threats from the Scots, in alliance with France, in the years up to 1560, and from the Spaniards in the later part of the century demonstrate that the possibility of invasion was always there, but English fears were sometimes exaggerated. The nightmare of a Franco-Imperial invasion, so vivid in Cromwell's mind in the later 1530s, did not come to pass, and the Armada of 1588 and subsequent Armadas of 1596 and 1597 never succeeded in landing troops on English soil. When invasions of the realm did occur, like that of the Scots in the north in 1513 or the Spaniards in Ireland in 1601, they were speedily crushed.

Wars and the threats of war cost money but Tudor monarchs, almost always pressed for cash, did at least avoid bankruptcies — unlike Philip II of Spain, theoretically the richest Christian monarch of the sixteenth century, who repudiated his debts on three occasions, in 1557, 1575 and 1596. The Crown's 'ordinary' revenues, the money coming to it year in year out from such sources as Crown lands, customs, the profits of justice and the rights of the sovereign as feudal overlord of England, did increase substantially in cash terms during the century, from about £100,000 a year in the 1520s to over £200,000 a year after the dissolution of the monasteries and to about £300,000 a year in the later part of Elizabeth's reign. These increases, however, did not keep pace with inflation and, except on rare occasions, notably during parts of the reigns of Henry VII and Henry VIII, ordinary revenue was never sufficient for expenditure. The Tudors did get help from parliament, mainly by means of the subsidy, a new tax on property introduced in the early years of Henry VIII's reign, and there has been much debate about whether or not this 'extraordinary' revenue came to be granted for the ordinary peacetime purposes of government rather than merely for emergencies.[58] What is certain is that the value of the subsidy fell sharply during the course of the century. It stood at about £140,000 at the beginning of Elizabeth's reign but was only about £85,000 at its end, mainly because the gentry commissioners, who made the assessments in the localities, were reluctant to tax their fellow gentlemen there at more than a small fraction of their true wealth.[59] Henry VII, Cromwell and Winchester all made significant efforts to raise the value of the Crown's revenues, but Burghley and Elizabeth, arch-conservatives in this field as in so many others, allowed the ordinary revenues of the Crown to fall sharply in real terms and acquiesced in the declining value of the subsidy.[60] By practising rigorous economy in expenditure they did keep the Crown solvent — even after nearly twenty years of war with Spain Elizabeth died not more than £350,000 in debt — but with more imaginative policies they could have done much to boost the Crown's revenue.

As far as the poorer members of the community were concerned it was not taxation demands which worried them — they were normally too poor to pay taxes — but the daily problems of feeding and clothing their families in an age when price increases outstripped wage rises and unemployment or underemployment was common. Here Tudor paternalism helped. Government measures to control the food supply and the elaboration of the poor law — by 1601 English legislation on the poor amounted to the most advanced national system in Europe — helped to ensure that there was little actual starvation, even in the dreadful years of the 1550s and 1590s.[61] It is true that at the end of the century private charity was still contributing a good deal more than national taxation to poor relief — Dr Slack has estimated that the respective figures were £25,000 and £10,000 *per annum* in 1610 — but already it was clear that taxation was increasing more rapidly than charitable endowments, and by the middle of the seventeenth century charitable benefactions and taxation each probably contributed about £100,000 a year to the relief of the poor. Tudor legislation, therefore, not only made some contribution to poor relief in the sixteenth century itself but held out considerable longer-term promise.[62]

These reflections suggest that, if we measure aims against achievements, Tudor government was on the whole a success story, and it can be argued that this is also the picture when we examine its strengths and weaknesses in a more general sense. Some historians have laid emphasis on what they see as notable weaknesses; Professor Stone, for example, entitled one of the sub-sections of an influential book, 'the instability of the Tudor polity',[63] but it is significant that two historians, Drs Penry Williams and John Guy, who have recently written large-scale analyses of the Tudor period, have taken a very different line. Both, as they themselves admit, started work on their books with ideas of the relative weakness of the Tudor state but were converted, during their researches, to ideas of relative strength.[64] They have both, therefore, come to agree broadly with Sir Geoffrey Elton, who, throughout his work, has emphasized the essential strength of Tudor institutions. In my own recent textbook on early modern England I concluded the Tudor section with a summary which balanced elements of both strength and weakness at the end of Elizabeth's reign.[65] Further reflection on the sixteenth century as a whole now leads me to alter the balance, the perspective, of the picture which I presented there. Above all, and unlike Stone, I would now stress the political *stability* of the Tudor state. Here we can return to the pictures in our introduction; the accession of Henry VII in victory in war in a highly unstable situation, and, in contrast, the quiet death of Elizabeth and the peaceful accession of James I to the throne of what was by then a stable realm.

The building and maintenance of stability is, perhaps, the dominant achievement of Tudor government and it can best be analysed in three periods.

The years 1485 to 1530 saw the creation of stability by Henry VII — that is the major theme of a recent perceptive study by Dr Grant[66] — and its maintenance by Henry VIII in his early years, described by Dr Davies as a 'period of internal tranquillity and confidence in the monarchy [unprecedented] since the reign of Edward III in the mid-fourteenth century'.[67] The second period, the years from 1530 to 1560, saw a series of revolutionary religious changes and economic, social and political upheavals. That was the period of the Reformation, in all its ramifications, most notably the repeated changes in religion which took place in the later years of Henry VIII, under Edward VI, under Mary, and at the beginning of Elizabeth's reign. There were also the most dramatic price increases of the century, some exceptionally bad harvests, a massive debasement of the coinage between 1542 and 1551 and a major trade crisis. In the political sphere an ageing king, arguably losing his grip on affairs, was succeeded in turn by a minor and by two women. That looks like *instability* with a vengeance, but immediate appearances are deceptive. Cromwell's governmental reforms in the 1530s created, as we have seen, a unitary and largely unified realm which survived him.

All of his reforms taken together, but especially his creation of a powerful Privy Council (a creation now recognized as the centrepiece of a much more complicated story than Elton initially supposed[68]), helped to ensure that, amidst all the dramatic changes, an underlying administrative stability was maintained. Somerset's threat to that stability — seen most clearly in his negative attitude towards the Privy Council — was a fundamental reason for his overthrow in 1549; but he had governed for too short a time to do fundamental damage. Northumberland restored administration through the Council and Mary maintained it.

In our third period, between 1560 and 1603, the Elizabethan regime, always fundamentally conservative, maintained and entrenched the underlying stability which had persisted throughout the decades of upheaval. Analyses of the Court, the Council, parliament and the patronage system have shown how this was done.[69] The 1590s certainly produced difficulties for the government but these must not be allowed to conceal the successes even of that decade.[70] After it was over the ease with which the Essex revolt was suppressed in 1601 and the smoothness of James's accession in 1603 bore witness to the essential strength and stability of Tudor government. James inherited a fully functioning polity. To repeat Dr Guy's happy judgment, Tudor government 'worked'.[71]

Notes

[1] For a good brief statement of the position, G.R. Elton, *The Tudor Constitution* (2nd ed., Cambridge, 1982), pp. 17-18.

[2] *Ibid.*, pp. 16-17.

[3] *Ibid.*, p. 14.

[4] A.G.R. Smith, *Servant of the Cecils* (1977), p. 108.

[5] See e.g. J. Murphy, 'The illusion of decline: the Privy Chamber 1547-1558', D.R. Starkey, ed., *The English Court* (1987), pp. 128-9, 138-9.

[6] *The Works of John Knox*, ed. D. Laing, iv (Edinburgh, 1855), pp. 373, 393.

[7] C. Haigh, *Elizabeth I* (1988), pp. 19-24.

[8] L.B. Smith, *Henry VIII: the mask of royalty* (1971).

[9] G.R. Elton, *Studies in Tudor and Stuart Politics and Government*, III (Cambridge, 1983), p.45.

[10] 'Journey through England and Scotland made by Lupold von Wedel in the years 1584 and 1585', *Transactions of the Royal Historical Society*, New Series, ix (1895), pp. 250-51.

[11] D.R. Starkey, ed., *The English Court* (1987), Chapter 1, Introduction.

[12] *Ibid.*, pp. 9-10.

[13] W.T. MacCaffrey, 'Place and Patronage in Elizabethan Politics', S.T. Bindoff, C.H. Williams, J. Hurstfield, eds, *Elizabethan Government and Society*, (1961), p.99.

[14] G.R. Elton, *Reform and Reformation* (1977); *Studies*, III (Cambridge, 1983), pp. 183 ff.

[15] E.W. Ives, *Anne Boleyn* (Oxford, 1986).

[16] D.R. Starkey, *The Reign of Henry VIII: Personalities and Politics* (1985).

[17] D. Hoak, *The King's Council in the Reign of Edward VI* (Cambridge, 1976).

[18] D. Loades, *The Reign of Mary Tudor* (1979).

[19] J. Hurstfield and A.G.R. Smith, eds, *Elizabethan People* (1972), p. 141.

[20] S. Adams, 'Faction, Clientage and Party: English Politics 1550-1603', *History Today*, December 1982, p. 34.

[21] Edmund Spenser, *Mother Hubbard's Tale*, lines 895-906.

[22] J. Hurstfield and A.G.R. Smith, eds, *Elizabethan People* (1972), p. 141.

[23] A.G.R. Smith, *The Government of Elizabethan England* (1967), pp. 24-5.

[24] D.R. Starkey, *The English Court* (1987), pp. 15 ff.

[25] For discussions of the central institutions of government see G.R. Elton *The Tudor Constitution* (2nd ed., Cambridge, 1982); P. Williams, *The Tudor Regime* (Oxford, 1979), part 1; A.G.R. Smith, *The Government of Elizabethan England* (1967), Chapter 4.

[26] R. Cecil, 'The State and Dignity of a Secretary of State's place ...', *Harleian Miscellany*, ii (1809), pp. 281-2.

[27] C. Read, *Mr Secretary Walsingham and Queen Elizabeth*, (3 vols, Oxford, 1925).

[28] P. Williams, *The Tudor Regime* (Oxford, 1979), p. 107.

[29] W.J. Jones, *The Elizabethan Court of Chancery* (Oxford, 1967), p. 8.

[30] A.G.R. Smith, 'The Secretariats of the Cecils, c. 1580-1612', *English Historical Review*, 83 (1968), pp. 481 ff; *Servant of the Cecils: the Life of Sir Michael Hickes* (1977), Chapter 2.

[31] D. Knowles, *The Religious Orders in England*, iii (Cambridge, 1959), pp. 241 ff.

[32] Contrast J.E. Neale, *Elizabeth I and her Parliaments* (2 vols, 1953, 1957) with M.A.R. Graves, *The Tudor Parliaments* (1985); *Elizabethan Parliaments* (1987) and G.R. Elton, *The Parliament of England 1559-81* (Cambridge, 1986).

[33] See the warnings of P. Collinson, 'Puritans, Men of Business and Elizabethan Parliaments', *Parliamentary History*, 7 (1988), pp. 187-211.

[34] G.R. Elton, *The Tudor Constitution* (2nd ed., Cambridge, 1982), p. 240.

[35] For details see P. Williams, *The Tudor Regime* (Oxford, 1979); G.R. Elton, *The Tudor Constitution* (2nd ed., Cambridge, 1982), Chapter 10; A.G.R. Smith, *The Government of Elizabethan England* (1967), Chapter 7.

[36] G. Scott Thomson, *Lords Lieutenant in the Sixteenth Century* (1923).

[37] W. Lambarde, *Eirenarcha* (1599 edition), pp. 608 ff.

[38] The last two offices were Tudor creations. On the constable see J.R. Kent, *The English Village Constable, 1580-1642* (Oxford, 1986).

[39] P. Williams, 'The Crown and the Counties', C. Haigh, ed., *The Reign of Elizabeth I* (1984), pp. 125 ff.

[40] A. Wall, 'Patterns of Politics in England, 1558-1625', *Historical Journal*, 31 (1988), pp. 947-63.

[41] See, e.g., G.R. Elton, *The Tudor Constitution* (2nd ed., Cambridge, 1982), pp. 15-16.

[42] J. Hurstfield and A.G.R. Smith, *Elizabethan People* (1972), p. 27.

[43] The best accounts are now P. Slack, *Poverty and Policy in Tudor and Stuart England* (1988) and J. Pound, *Poverty and Vagrancy in Tudor England* (2nd ed., 1986).

[44] P. Williams, *The Tudor Regime* (Oxford, 1979), pp. 185 ff. has an excellent brief discussion.

[45] J. Hurstfield, 'Was there a Tudor Despotism after all?', *Freedom, Corruption and Government in*

Elizabethan England (1973), pp. 23 ff.

[46] See the convincing reply by G.R. Elton, 'The Rule of Law in Sixteenth Century England', *Studies*, I (Cambridge, 1974), pp. 260 ff.

[47] G.R. Elton, *Policy and Police*, (Cambridge, 1972).

[48] R.W. Heinze, *The Proclamations of the Tudor Kings* (Cambridge, 1976).

[49] G.R. Elton, *The Tudor Revolution in Government* (Cambridge, 1953).

[50] See R.B. Wernham in *English Historical Review*, 71 (1956), pp. 93-4 and the debate by Drs G.L. Harriss and P. Williams on the one hand and Elton on the other in *Past and Present*, numbers 25 (July 1963), 29 (December 1964), 31 (July 1965) and 32 (December 1965).

[51] The most important recent criticisms are in C. Coleman and D.R. Starkey, eds, *Revolution Reassessed* (Oxford, 1986) and D.R. Starkey, ed., *The English Court* (1987).

[52] A.L. Brown, *The Governance of Late Medieval England 1272-1461* (1989), p. 2.

[53] D.R. Starkey, 'Introduction', *The English Court*, ed., D.R. Starkey (1987), pp. 1 ff.

[54] J.D. Alsop, 'The Structure of Early Tudor Finance, c. 1509-1558', C. Coleman and D.R. Starkey, eds, *Revolution Reassessed* (Oxford, 1986), pp. 135 ff.

[55] C. Coleman, 'Artifice or Accident? The Reorganization of the Exchequer of Receipt, c. 1554-1572', *Ibid.*, pp. 163 ff.

[56] See his review of Starkey's *English Court* in *Historical Journal*, 31 (1988), pp. 425-34.

[57] C. Haigh, 'The Recent Historiography of the English Reformation', *Historical Journal*, 25 (1982), pp. 995 ff.; A.G. Dickens, 'The Early Expansion of Protestantism in England', *Archiv für Reformationsgeschichte*, (1987), pp. 187 ff.

[58] The latest major contribution to the debate is by J.D. Alsop, 'The theory and practice of Tudor taxation', *English Historical Review*, 97 (1982), pp. 1 ff.

[59] R.S. Schofield, 'Taxation and the political limits of the Tudor state', C. Cross, D. Loades, and J.J. Scarisbrick, eds, *Law and Government under the Tudors* (Cambridge, 1988), pp. 227 ff.

[60] P. Williams, *The Tudor Regime* (Oxford, 1979), pp. 70 ff; A.G.R. Smith, *The Emergence of a Nation State* (1984), pp. 118-19.

[61] A.B. Appleby, *Famine in Tudor and Stuart England* (Liverpool, 1978).

[62] P. Slack, *Poverty and Policy in Tudor and Stuart England* (1988), pp. 169 ff.

[63] L. Stone, *The Causes of the English Revolution 1529-1642* (1972), pp. 58-67.

[64] P. Williams, *The Tudor Regime* (Oxford, 1979), pp. 459-60; J. Guy, *Tudor England* (Oxford; 1988), p. 513 note 47.

[65] A.G.R. Smith, *The Emergence of a Nation State* (1984), pp. 248-50.

[66] A. Grant, *Henry VII* (Lancaster Pamphlet, 1985).

[67] C.S.L. Davies, *Peace, Print and Protestantism 1450-1558* (Paladin ed., 1977), p. 157.

[68] J. Guy, 'The Privy Council: Revolution or Evolution?' C. Coleman and D.R. Starkey, eds, *Revolution Reassessed* (Oxford, 1986), pp. 59 ff.

[69] G.R. Elton, *Studies*, III (Cambridge, 1983), pp. 3 ff., 21 ff., 38 ff.; S. Adams, 'Eliza enthroned? The Court and its Politics', C. Haigh, ed., *The Reign of Elizabeth I* (1984), pp. 62-3; A.G.R. Smith, *The Emergence of a Nation State* (1984), pp. 121 ff.

[70] Smith, *Ibid.*, p. 249.

[71] J. Guy, *Tudor England* (Oxford, 1988), p. 458.

Bibliography

Recent general works which contain discussions of Tudor government and governmental institutions, both central and local, include C.S.L. Davies, *Peace, Print and Protestantism, 1450-1558* (1976); P. Williams, *The Tudor Regime* (Oxford, 1979); G.R. Elton, *The Tudor Constitution* (2nd ed., Cambridge 1982); A.G.R. Smith, *The Emergence of a Nation State: the Commonwealth of England 1529-1660* (1984); J. Guy, *Tudor England* (Oxford, 1988); and C. Haigh, *Elizabeth I* (1988). Elton's collected essays, *Studies in Tudor and Stuart Politics and Government* (3 vols, Cambridge, 1974-83) contain much important material.

Important works on the Court, a growth point in present-day Tudor historiography, are D.R. Starkey, ed., *The English Court: from the Wars of the Roses to the Civil War* (1987); D. Loades, *The Tudor Court* (1986); G.R. Elton, 'Tudor Government: the Points of Contact. III. The Court', *Studies*, III (Cambridge, 1983); and S. Adams, 'Eliza enthroned? The Court and its Politics', C. Haigh, ed., *The Reign of Elizabeth I* (1984).

On politics, patronage and faction the classic essay is J.E. Neale's 1948 British Academy lecture, 'The Elizabethan Political Scene', reprinted in his *Essays in Elizabethan History* (1958). Since then many works have discussed factional politics and the patronage machine in general and specific episodes in detail. E.W. Ives, *Faction in Tudor England* (H.A. New Appreciations in History, 6, 2nd ed., 1986), is a good survey. For somewhat different interpretations there are D.R. Starkey, 'From Feud to Faction: English Politics c.1450-1550', *History Today*, 32 (1982) and S. Adams, 'Faction, Clientage and Party, 1550-1603', *History Today*, 32 (1982). There is important discussion of specific episodes in G.R. Elton, *Reform and Reformation: England 1509-58* (1977); E.W. Ives, *Anne Boleyn* (Oxford, 1986); L.B. Smith, *Henry VIII: the mask of royalty* (1971); J.J. Scarisbrick, *Henry VIII* (1968); D.R. Starkey, *The Reign of Henry VIII: Personalities and Politics* (1985); D.E. Hoak, *The King's Council in the Reign of Edward VI* (Cambridge, 1976); D.M. Loades, *The Reign of Mary Tudor* (1979); W.T. MacCaffrey, *The Shaping of the Elizabethan Regime: Elizabethan Politics 1558-72* (1969); *Queen Elizabeth and the Making of policy, 1572-88* (Princeton, 1981); and A.G.R. Smith, *Servant of the Cecils, the Life of Sir Michael Hickes, 1543-1612* (1977). An excellent survey of recent work on local politics, patronage and faction is A. Wall, 'Patterns of Politics in England, 1558-1625', *Historical Journal*, 31 (1988).

Specific aspects of central administration are covered in J. Guy, *The Cardinal's Court* (1977), the fundamental work on the early history of Star Chamber; W.J. Jones, *The Elizabethan Court of Chancery* (Oxford, 1967); and J. Hurstfield, *The Queen's Wards* (1958). A detailed study of the Council is badly needed. At the moment the best introduction is G.R. Elton, 'Tudor Government: the Points of Contact. II. The Council', *Studies*, III (Cambridge, 1983). On taxation J.D. Alsop, 'The Theory and Practice of Tudor Taxation', *English Historical Review*, 97 (1982), and R.S. Schofield, 'Taxation and the political limits of the Tudor State', C. Cross, D. Loades, J.J. Scarisbrick, eds, *Law and Government under the Tudors* (Cambridge, 1988), are important essays. R.W. Heinze and J.A. Youngs have respectively written detailed studies of *The Proclamations of the Tudor Kings* (Cambridge, 1976) and *The Proclamations of the Tudor Queens* (Cambridge, 1976).

Neale's work on parliament, *Elizabeth I and her Parliaments* (2 vols., 1953, 1957), has been strongly challenged and partially demolished by G.R. Elton, *The*

Parliament of England 1559-81 (Cambridge, 1986) and M.A.R. Graves, *The Tudor Parliaments* (1985); *Elizabethan Parliaments* (1987). Very recently P. Collinson, in his Neale lecture, 'Puritans, Men of Business and Elizabethan Parliaments', *Parliamentary History*, 7 (1988), has warned against pushing 'revisionism' too far.

On local government G. Scott Thomson, *Lords Lieutenant in the Sixteenth Century* (1923), is still the best study of that important office. Insights into the growing work of the justices of the peace can be gained from William Lambarde's *Eirenarcha* (1599 edition), while J.R. Kent, *The English Village Constable, 1580-1642* (Oxford, 1986), helps to illustrate the growth in the importance of the parish which took place during the Tudor period. Among the best recent studies of specific counties are P. Clark, *English Provincial Society from the Reformation to the Revolution: Religion, Politics and Society in Kent, 1540-1640* (1977); D. MacCulloch, *Suffolk and the Tudors: Politics and Religion in an English County, 1500-1600* (Oxford, 1986); and A. Hassell Smith, *County and Court: Government and Politics in Norfolk, 1558-1603* (Oxford, 1974).

Government attitudes towards the poor can now be best followed in P. Slack, *Poverty and Policy in Tudor and Stuart England* (1988), and J. Pound, *Poverty and Vagrancy in Tudor England*, (2nd ed., 1986), while discussions of town government can be found in P. Clark and P. Slack, eds, *Crisis and Order in English Towns, 1500-1700* (1972); *English Towns in Transition, 1500-1700* (Oxford, 1976).

J. Hurstfield's defence of the idea of Tudor despotism 'Was there a Tudor despotism after all?', *Freedom, Corruption and Government in Elizabethan England* (1973) was strongly and convincingly attacked by G.R. Elton, 'The Rule of Law in 16th Century England', *Studies*, I (Cambridge, 1974). Elton's *Policy and Police: the Enforcement of the Reformation in the Age of Thomas Cromwell* (Cambridge, 1972), demonstrates that Henry VIII and Cromwell stuck rigidly to the letter of the law in the enforcement of the Reformation.

Elton's famous book, *The Tudor Revolution in Government* (Cambridge, 1953), launched a debate about continuity and change in Tudor administration which is still in progress, but recent contributions in C. Coleman and D. Starkey, eds, *Revolution Reassessed: Revisions in the History of Tudor Government and Administration* (Oxford, 1986) and D. Starkey, ed., *The English Court* (1987) reinforce the doubts about Elton's thesis which have been expressed since soon after he wrote the book.